Fernando Sor

Selected Studies
Arranged for Electric Bass

I0801536

Paul Ballam-Cross

WWW.MELBAY.COM

Introduction

Through teaching both bass guitar and classical guitar, I found that there was very little accessible solo bass repertoire for the beginner or intermediate player. Tapping into some of the classical guitar material that I knew well, I reworked some of Fernando Sor's studies for the bass guitar.

Fernando Sor's music is perfectly composed for the six-string classical guitar, so some changes were required in order to transcribe his pieces for the four-string bass. Nonetheless, I chose pieces that didn't require substantial alterations –other than some key changes– to be playable. In the spirit of Sor's original intention for these pieces to be used as educational material, I arranged several works for two basses, perhaps to be played by teacher and student.

The material in this book is drawn from Sor's several sets of studies (or études) for the guitar. These include his *24 Leçons progressives,* Op. 31, *24 Exercices très faciles,* Op. 35, *24 Petites pièces progressives,* Op. 44a, and *Introduction à l'étude de la guitare,* Op. 60. All of these collections and the pieces within them have been frequently recorded by guitarists. Brian Jeffery, author of the biography *Fernando Sor: Composer and Guitarist*, notes that in all of these pieces, "Sor's craftsmanship is superb . . . his aim is always a musical experience, a shape, a form, a structure, and even his simplest pieces are beautifully written. Whether a piece is called a study, a lesson, or an exercise is not so important; what matters is that this is music by a fine musician".

Likewise, whether a bass player using this book intends to use it for teaching, practice or just for fun, I hope that the end result is enjoyable to play!

Fernando Sor – a Brief Biography

Born in Barcelona in 1778, Fernando Sor was sent at a young age to be a chorister in the monastery of Montserrat. He was trained here as an all-around musician, studying composition and counterpoint before enrolling in military school.

He later became an army lieutenant, fighting in the war of the 1790s against the French, before turning more seriously to music and becoming famous in Barcelona as both a performer and as a composer for the guitar.

Despite Sor's writing of anti-French songs in protest, Napoleon Bonaparte's invasion of Spain in 1808 led to Sor taking an administrative role in the occupying government. After Wellington's victory at the Battle of Vitoria in 1813, the French retreated and Sor found himself forced to leave Spain, being labelled an *afrancesado* (those who either supported or did not act against the French).

Travelling widely after this, Sor initially found himself in Paris, before turning to London. Here, he found much fame and fortune; Jeffery quotes one review from 1820 which notes that "Mr. Sor's vocal compositions have gained such favour that a new set of arietts, from his pen, causes almost as much sensation as the publication of a new novel by the author of *Waverley* [Sir Walter Scott]". Sor's ballet music was equally successful; his *Cendrillon*, already successful in London and Paris, was performed at the opening of the Bolshoi Theatre in Moscow in 1823.

Sor married the dancer Félicité Hullin, who received an invitation to perform and work in Moscow. Following her to Russia, Sor taught, composed, and performed there for three years before their separation led to his return to Paris in 1827. Primarily composing and teaching during this time, it was in Paris that he wrote much of the material that appears in this book. He died in 1839 of tongue cancer.

Editorial Commentary

I have chosen to include a fairly limited number of fingerings throughout the pieces so as to allow the player to read the notes more easily. Much of the material in this book is quite playable with no fingerings as a guide but, in more complex passages, I have nonetheless included some suggestions. These fingerings should be taken as suggestions only, as alternatives are quite possible.

In some of these pieces there are pairs of notes to which I have added brackets. These notes are intended for beginning players, who can ignore the bracketed notes without losing the effect of the piece. More advanced players can play the pair as written.

These pieces are also arranged roughly in order of difficulty. This is a very subjective process, so any player diligently reading through is encouraged to explore other pieces in the book.

The last few pieces in this book are all duets. As mentioned earlier, these could be performed by a student and teacher, or perhaps by two students. The level of difficulty of the melodic part of the duets is a little higher than the rest of the book, and they are intended as "extension" material.

Many thanks to Dr Genesta Nicolson and Joel Woods for their assistance in proofreading this book.

Dr. Paul Ballam-Cross
Brisbane Australia, April 2021

Bibliography

Jeffery, Brian (n.d.). *Fernando Sor (1778-1839)* biography. London, Tecla Editions.

Jeffery, Brian (n.d.). *Fernando Sor – Life and Music.* London, Tecla Editions.

Jeffery, Brian (1994). *Fernando Sor: Composer and Guitarist.* London, Tecla Editions.

Page, Christopher (2013). "New light on the London years of Fernando Sor, 1815-1822". *Early Music*, Volume 41, Issue 4, pp. 557-569.

Contents

Fernando Sor (1778-1839)

Lesson No. 1

from *Introduction à l'étude de la guitare*, Op. 60

Lesson No. 2

from *Introduction à l'étude de la guitare*, Op. 60

29
35

Lesson No. 3

from *Introduction à l'étude de la guitare*, Op. 60

17

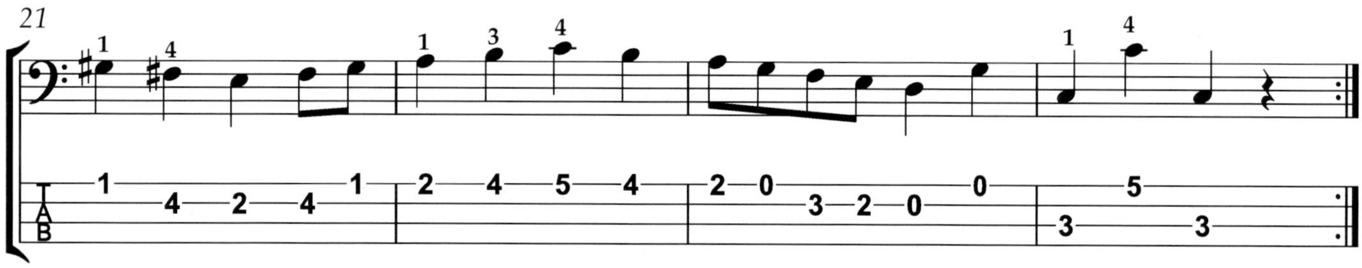
21

Lesson No. 10

from *Introduction à l'étude de la guitare*, Op. 60

This page has been left blank to avoid an awkward page turn.

Lesson No. 11

from *Introduction à l'étude de la guitare*, Op. 60

25
29
D.C. al Fine

Study No. 1

from *24 Petites pièces progressives*, Op. 44a

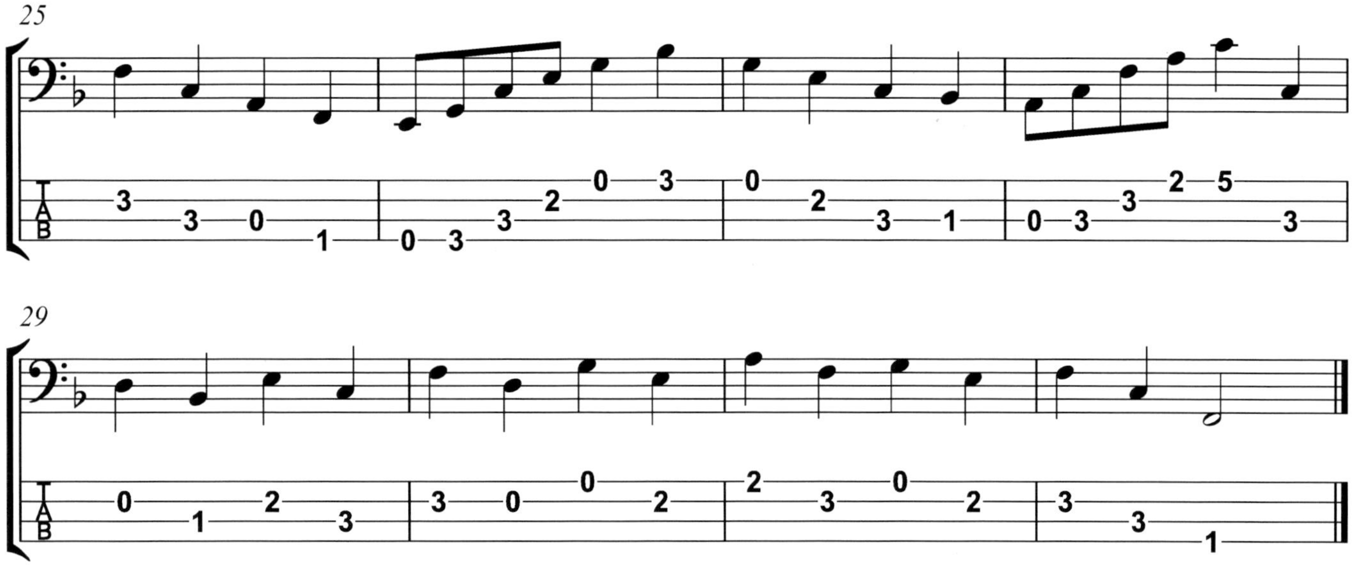
25
29

Lesson No. 6

from *Introduction à l'étude de la guitare*, Op. 60

D.S. al Fine

Lesson No. 18

from *24 Leçons progressives*, Op. 31

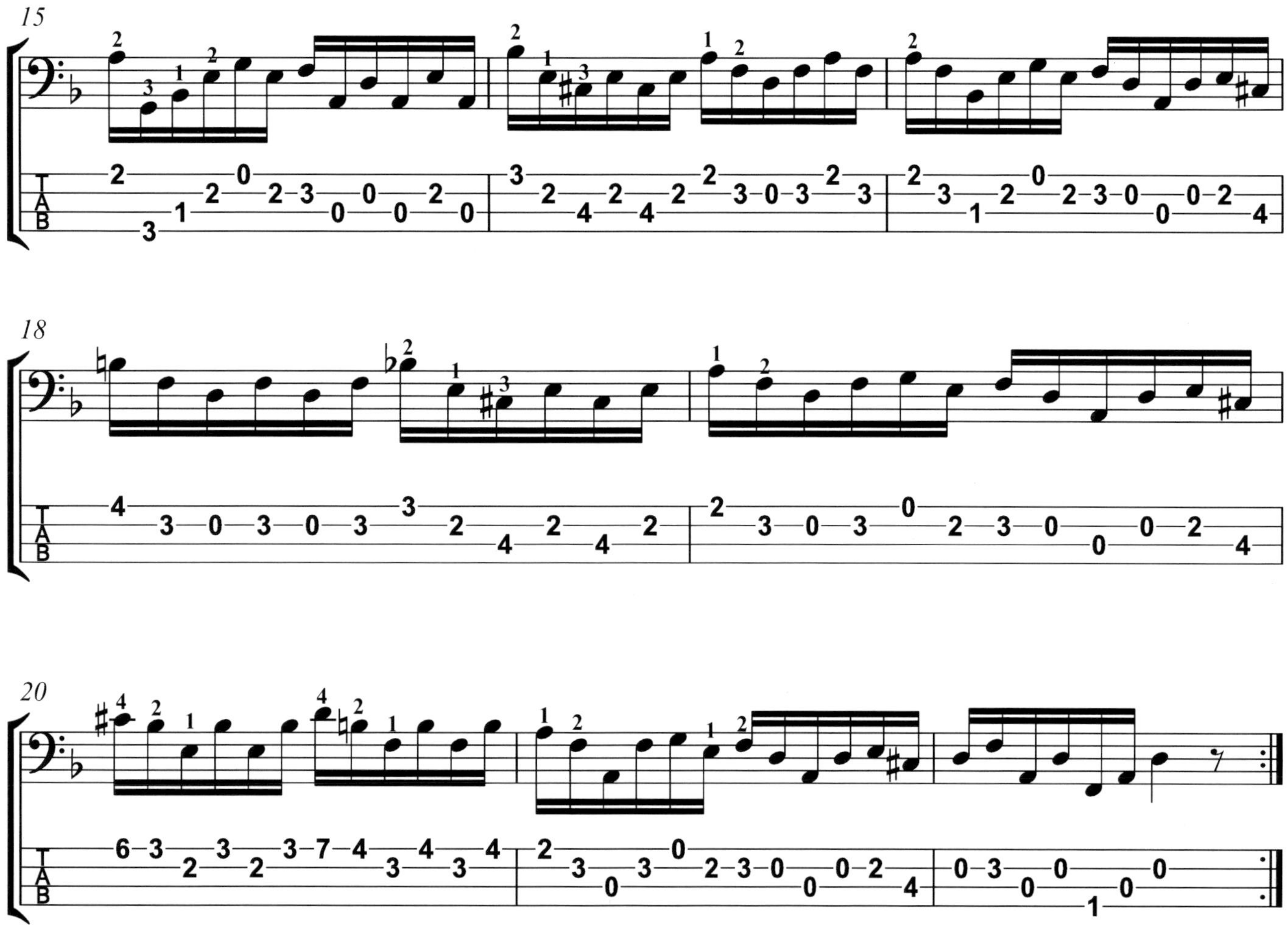

Study No. 2

from *24 Petites pièces progressives*, Op. 44a

25
29
33
37

Study No. 14

from *24 Petites pièces progressives*, Op. 44a

Tempo di minuetto moderato

21
25
TAB

Lesson No. 4

from *Introduction à l'étude de la guitare*, Op. 60

This page has been left blank to avoid an awkward page turn.

Lesson No. 5

from *Introduction à l'étude de la guitare*, Op. 60

25
29
33
37

Lesson No. 17

from *Introduction à l'étude de la guitare*, Op. 60

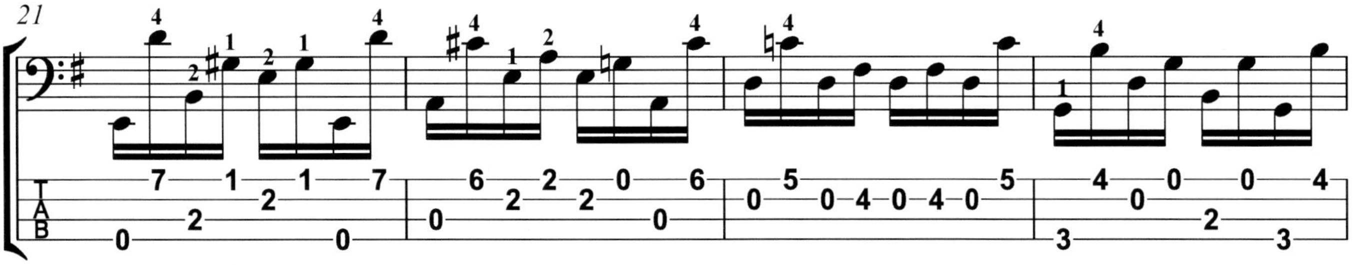
21

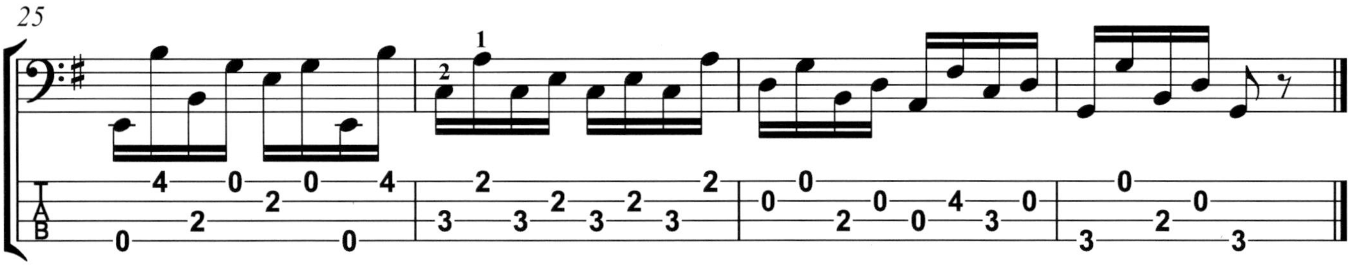
25

Study No. 6

from *24 Petites pièces progressives*, Op. 44a

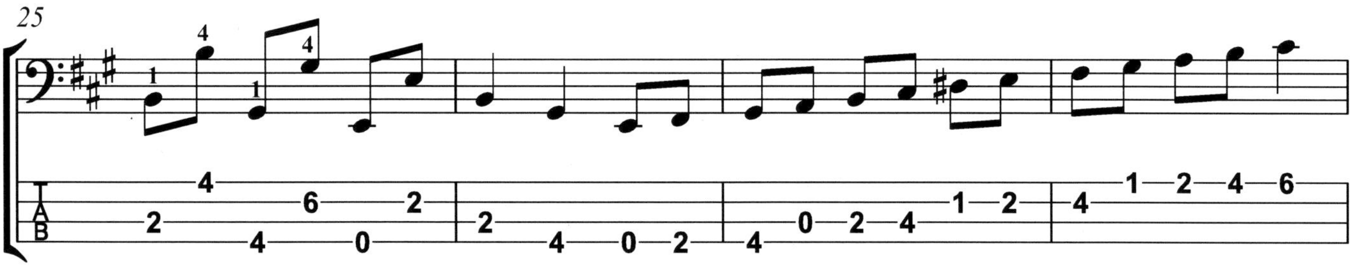

Study No. 2 - Bass 1

from *24 Exercices très faciles*, Op. 35

Andantino

Study No. 2 - Bass 2

from *24 Exercices très faciles*, Op. 35

Andantino

Study No. 2

from *24 Exercices très faciles*, Op. 35

Lesson No. 14 - Bass 1

from *24 Leçons progressives*, Op. 31

Lesson No. 14 - Bass 2

from *24 Leçons progressives*, Op. 31

Andantino

25
29
33

Lesson No. 14

from *24 Leçons progressives*, Op. 31

13
17
21

This page has been left blank to avoid an awkward page turn.

Lesson No. 11 - Bass 1

from *24 Leçons progressives*, Op. 31

Lesson No. 11 - Bass 2

from *24 Leçons progressives*, Op. 31

Lesson No. 11

from *24 Leçons progressives*, Op. 31

13
17
21

Study No. 15 - Bass 1

from *24 Petites pièces progressives*, Op. 44a

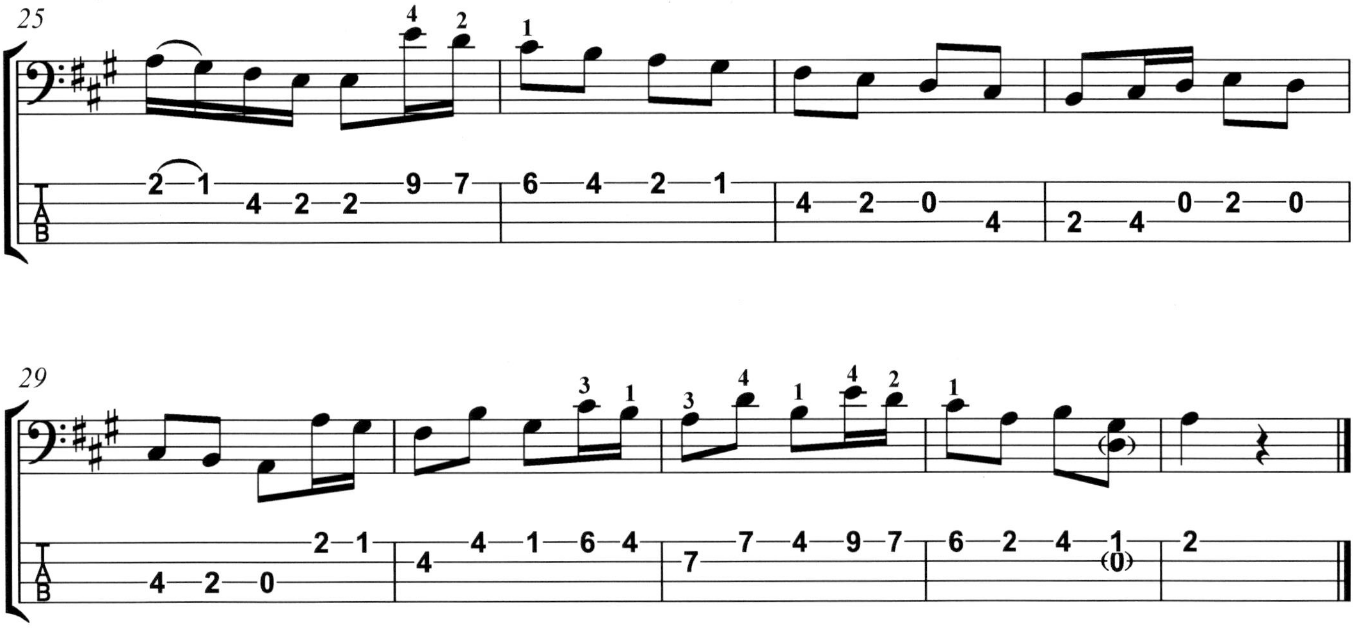

Study No. 15 - Bass 2

from *24 Petites pièces progressives*, Op. 44a

Andante

25
T
A
B
0
0 2 4
0 4 2 0
4 2 0 2 4

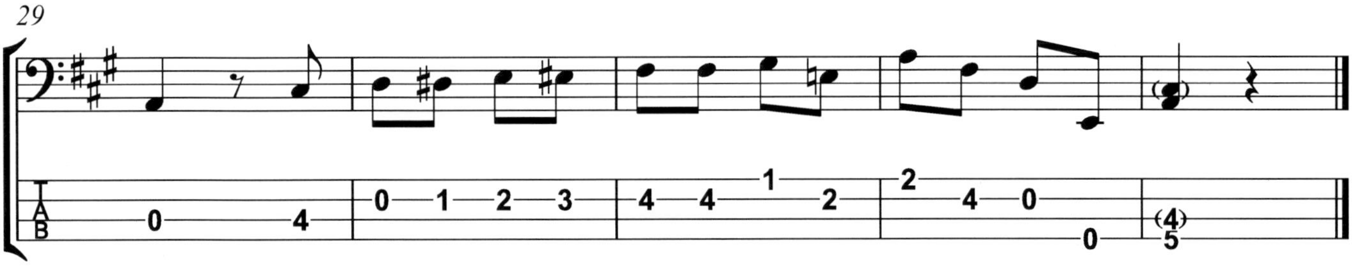
29
T
A
B
0 4
0 1 2 3
4 4 1 2
2 4 0 0
(4)
5

Study No. 15

from *24 Petites pièces progressives*, Op. 44a

13
17
21

25
29

About the Author

Paul Ballam-Cross
Photo Courtesy of Ash Heard

Dr. Paul Ballam-Cross is a writer, classical guitarist, and bassist. He has completed a Bachelor of Music in Performance majoring in classical guitar, and a Doctor of Philosophy, majoring in musicology. Paul is a regular reviewer for *Limelight Magazine*, as Australian website and monthly classical music and arts magazine, and is a casual lecturer at the University of Queensland. His research interests include exploring both transcriptions for guitar and the methods used in creating them, as well as the intersections between popular music and the internet.

Other Mel Bay Bass Books

5-String Bass Scale Chart (Dozier)
5-String Bass Scale Wall Chart (Dozier)
100 Fretless Bass Workouts (Matheos)
50 Modal Slap Bass Workouts (Matheos)
100 R & B Soul Grooves for Bass (Matheos)
100 Rock & Roll Workouts for Bass (Matheos)
50 Two-Hand Tapping Workouts for Electric Bass (Matheos)
Bass Chart of Scales and Modes (Roth)
Bass Warm-Ups (Matheos)
Bass Scale Chart (C. Christiansen)
Bass Scale Wall Chart (C. Christiansen)
Bass Scales in Tablature (Betts)
Classical and Contemporary Studies for Bass Guitar (Bottesini/Isbin)
Complete Book of Bass Essentials (Brunel)
Drum and Bass Synchronicity: The Ultimate Rhythm Section Workout (Prushko/Dozier)
Electric Bass Position Studies (Filiberto)
Encyclopedia of Bass Arpeggios (Palermo)
Encyclopedia of Scales & Modes for Electric Bass (Roth)
Improvising on Electric Bass (Raso)
Jazz Scales for Bass (C. Christiansen/Farmer)
Killer Technique: Bass Guitar (C. Bay)
Learn to Burn: Electric Bass (Dozier)
Learn to Burn: 5-String Bass (Dozier)
Note Reading Studies for Bass (Evans)
Power Tools for 5-String Bass (Cockfield)
Rock Bass Technique (Hiland)
Scale Studies for Bass (Monoxelos)
Slappin': A Complete Study of the Slap Technique for Bass (Ensign)
Soloing on Electric Bass (Raso)
The Literate Bassist (Paterno)
Time Signature Studies for Bass (Rainey)
Walking Bass (Rector)
Walking Jazz Lines for Bass (Hungerford)
5-String Bass Chord Wall Chart (Dozier)
Bass Chord Picture Book (W. Bay)
Bass Chords Made Easy (W. Bay)
Bass Chords Qwikguide (W. Bay)
Bass Fingerstyle Funk Grooves Made Easy (Matheos)